Science Fair Success
with Plants

Phyllis J. Perry

Enslow Publishers, Inc.

40 Industrial Road   PO Box 38
Box 398   Aldershot
Berkeley Heights, NJ 07922   Hants GU12 6BP
USA   UK

http://www.enslow.com

For David

Library of Congress Cataloging-in-Publication Data

Perry, Phyllis Jean.
    Science fair success with plants / Phyllis J. Perry.
        p. cm. — (Science fair success)
    Summary: Details twenty-five experiments demonstrating the structure,
environmental needs, and life processes of plants.
    Includes bibliographical references (p.   ) and index.
    ISBN 0-7660-1170-4
    1. Botany projects—Juvenile literature. [1. Botany projects.
2. Experiments.] I. Title. II. Series.
QK526.P47   1999
580'.78—dc21   98-25944
                                           CIP
                                           AC

To Our Readers:
All Internet addresses in this book were active and appropriate when we went to press.
Any comments or suggestions can be sent by e-mail to Comments@enslow.com or to
the address on the back cover.

Illustration Credits: Stephen F. Delisle

Photo Credits: © Corel Corporation

Cover Illustration: © Corel Corporation

Contents

Introduction

Scientists are always looking at the world and trying to understand how things work. One of the most interesting fields of scientific endeavor is biology, the study of living things. Botany, which is the study of plants, is a branch of biology.

In our world, there are more than three hundred fifty thousand kinds of plants. Studying even a small number of these plants could keep a person busy for a long time. The investigations in this book will give you some general information on how to begin your study of the world of plants.

Botanists study the structure and environments of plants. As a result of their initial observations, they may formulate a hypothesis—an educated, scientific explanation that has yet to be proved. Then, the scientists look at their subjects even more carefully, taking and recording measurements, noting their observations, and carrying out experiments. These activities may prove or disprove the initial hypothesis.

In this book, you will carry out investigations and engage in activities that will help you learn more about the plant world. Perhaps you will become involved in an experiment just for the fun of it. Maybe you are simply curious and want to try some hands-on activities. You might get involved in botany as a part of a unit of study at school. Or perhaps you are being asked to consider entering a project in a science fair and think that experimenting with plants would be interesting.

Whatever the reason, this book may prove helpful to you. It includes a number of investigations that involve simple and inexpensive materials. Many of these materials will be available around your home or at school. Each investigation is outlined in sufficient detail so that you will know how to gather materials and how to get started. You are encouraged to make careful observations and to take detailed notes.

When scientists undertake experiments, they use the scientific method. There is more than one way to approach scientific questions, because each problem has conditions that dictate part of the method to be used. But you should consider six basic steps in each investigation: purpose, hypothesis, procedure, observations and data collecting, results, and conclusions.

The purpose may be stated as a question to be answered by your investigation. This question may arise out of observations or from background reading. The hypothesis is an educated guess about the answer to the question. It is often formulated after some of the initial reading on a topic is done but before a detailed investigation is carried out.

The procedure involves a plan for research through reading, talking with others, observing, and experimenting. Collecting the data requires care with variables, controls, notes, logbooks, and repetitions. After the experimentation and gathering of data, the results can be listed. Then, the scientist can look back at the hypothesis and initial purpose of the project and make a cautious conclusion.

Although including several repetitions and taking an average helps the experimenter feel more sure of the conclusions drawn, there is the possibility that some experiments will not turn out as planned. When this occurs, valuable learning can still take place as the experimenter tries to figure out why the results were not as expected and decides whether to change protocols and try again.

This book begins with an examination of plant structure, moves to a consideration of a plant's environmental needs, and then concludes with studying the life processes of plants. Each experiment begins with a question. Carefully following the outlined procedures will help you find the answers to these questions.

At the end of each investigation is a section with suggestions for further explorations. Some of these topics may give you an idea to develop your own original science fair project. You may also have your own further questions after finishing an investigation and want to plan another experiment. Bring your plan to a teacher, parent, or other adult for suggestions before launching into another project.

Before you begin any investigation, read through the entire activity from beginning to end. The information will help you understand the scope of the investigation and the time that will be involved, the materials that will be needed, and the procedures that should be followed. In some cases, the investigation has several parts. You might want to try one or all of the parts suggested.

Always use common sense. Sometimes you will be using a knife or scissors, an electrical source, or an oven. Safety must be of primary concern. A few projects may require adult supervision, and these will be clearly marked. You may be handling decaying leaves or a piece of moldy bread. Be sure to clean up your work area and equipment and to wash your hands thoroughly with soap and water after handling specimens and materials.

At the end of the book is a list of suggestions for further reading and sites on the World Wide Web that you might want to consult for additional information. The books listed should be easy to locate at your bookstore or library or through interlibrary loan. Although the Web sites were up and running at the time of publication, some may have been dropped, some may have been updated, and others may have been added.

These investigations should be fun. Perhaps they will lead to a lifelong interest in the fascinating field of botany.

Part I

Plant Structure

Plants can be classified into major groups. Simple plants lack roots, stems, and leaves. Green algae are an example of simple plants. Seedless complex plants, such as ferns, horsetails, and club mosses, have tubes that run through the stems between the leaves and the roots. Complex plants with seeds are those plants that have either cones (such as pine, fir, and spruce trees) or those that have flowers. Flowering plants can be further divided into monocotyledons (such as grasses, tulips, irises, lilies, and orchids) or dicotyledons (such as roses, geraniums, and beans).

This first section is designed to reveal the basic structure of plants: their roots, stems, leaves, flowers, and seeds.

Investigation 1

How do roots grow?

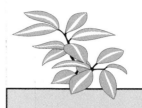

Photosynthesis is the process that enables plant leaves to turn sunlight into energy for the plant. These leaves can be thought of as food factories. Chlorophyll in the chloroplast cells of the leaves allow water and carbon dioxide to combine and form a molecule of sugar. Energy is stored in the sugar molecule.

Plants get most of their nutrients through the soil and through their root systems. Perhaps you have wondered just how plant roots grow—Do they grow from the top of the root or from the tip of the root?

Materials

* popcorn kernels
* small, plastic tumbler
* water
* paper towels
* plastic box with cover (or baking pan with plastic wrap)
* magnifying glass
* ruler
* notebook and pen
* permanent marker
* glass jar with lid

Put several kernels of popcorn in a small, plastic tumbler. Add sufficient water to cover them and let the kernels sit overnight. The kernels will soak up much water and swell.

Lay the kernels on wet paper towels in a plastic box. Put the cover on the box and observe the kernels several times a day, recording your observations. If the paper towels start to dry, sprinkle them with water. (You can also use a baking pan and cover the top with clear plastic wrap.) Keep the box (or pan) in a warm, dark place.

Seeds change very fast. In a starter garden like this one inside clear plastic, you can watch daily and see what is going on. What happens to the size of the seed? Does the skin remain intact? In a few days, do roots push out from one end? What sprouts from the other end?

In your popcorn garden, you may notice white fuzz covering the roots. Observe this covering by using a magnifying glass. You will see that the fuzz is really hundreds of hairs. Each of these root hairs is just one cell shaped like a long, thin tube. Most of the water taken into the plant comes in through these hairs. (It is also possible that in very warm, moist conditions, mold will grow on the roots in the popcorn garden. Be alert to this.)

The roots of your popcorn seed may grow as much in one week as you grew all last year. Measure the length of the roots

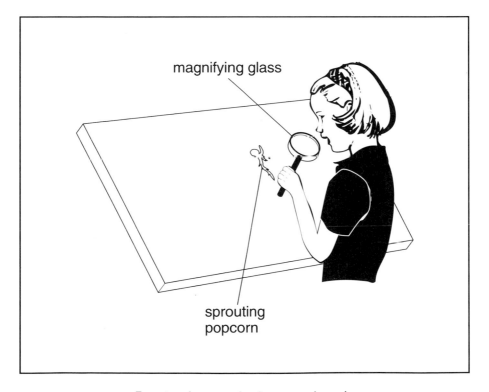

Examine the growth of popcorn kernels.

of your seeds after three days. Wait three more days, then measure again. Each time you measure, keep a record in your notebook. Include the date, time, and length of the root from its tip to the seed.

When the roots have grown about three inches, use a permanent marker and mark the roots of two plants with dots spaced one-quarter inch apart.

Roll up sheets of wet paper towel and arrange them against the sides of a clear glass jar. Add a little water to the bottom of the jar so that the towels can continually soak it up. Put the two marked popcorn plants with their roots hanging down between the glass jar and the wet paper towels.

Cover the jar and put it on a windowsill. Add water as needed to keep the paper towels damp. After a few days you

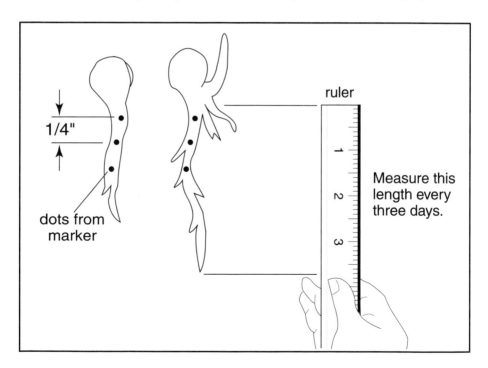

Measure the length of the roots every three days.

will be able to observe which part of the root is growing. Is it the tip or the base? What happens to the space between the dots? All roots grow in this way.

A chemical called a hormone forms in the root tip when the seeds germinate and makes the root grow longer. You can buy a similar chemical in stores that sell plants. It is a root promoter, and used as directed, it will speed root growth in plants.

Further Explorations

Many ideas may occur to you for further experimentation. Try them! For example, do hydroponic plants (that grow in a liquid nutrient solution) make fewer roots than terrestrial plants?

Investigation 2

How does water move throughout a plant?

Plants need water, minerals, carbon dioxide, and oxygen to survive. In humans, a circulatory system transports blood. Some plants also have a transport system. They are called vascular plants and have vessels like miniature tubes or straws. Other plants such as algae, mosses, and lichens are nonvascular. They have no tubes, and minerals and water must come in direct contact with the outer cells.

The movement of water—up and down, from soil to plant—is through tubes called xylem. Sugars and starches to be used by the plant cells move through tubes called phloem. You can see the difference between these tubes by using a carrot and colored water.

Use red food coloring to dye the water in a tall, clear jar. Place a small carrot into the jar and leave it there for forty-eight hours.

Then use a knife (**with adult supervision**) to slice off the

Materials

* red food coloring
* water
* 2 tall, clear jars
* small carrot
* knife
* magnifying glass
* blue food coloring
* masking tape
* white carnation
* clear plastic wrap
* notebook and pen
* centimeter ruler
* 3 stalks of celery, with leaves
* 3 tall, clear drinking glasses
* measuring cup
* tablespoon
* salt
* sugar
* 3 plates

top of the carrot about an inch from the top. Next, **ask an adult** to slice the carrot lengthwise.

Look at the carrot carefully through a magnifying glass. You will be able to see that the center of the carrot is now red. This area is the xylem that carries water up and down the plant. The phloem, which carries food, does not turn red. It remains orange. Can you figure out why?

You can learn more about the movement of water in vascular plants by studying carnations and stalks of celery.

Get two tall, clear jars. Add fresh water to each, putting exactly the same amount of liquid in each jar. In one jar, add red food coloring. Add plenty of coloring (thirty drops) so that the water is a deep red color. To the other jar of water, add enough blue food coloring to make the water a deep blue. Put the jars side by side. Use a piece of tape to mark each jar showing the level of the water.

Take a white carnation and **ask an adult** to use a sharp knife to split the lower half of the stem up the middle. Put one half of the stem into the jar of blue water and the other half into the jar of red water. Use clear plastic wrap over the tops of the jars and around the stem to reduce evaporation.

Each day, check to see whether the white carnation is changing color. In your notebook, record the time, date, and what you observe. Each day check the level of the water. Using a centimeter ruler, record how far the water level has dropped.

In much the same way that color moves up the carnation, water travels to the top of giant sequoia trees. It moves by capillary action and transpiration. Transpiration is the evaporation of water vapor from the surface of the green plant tissues.

You have observed capillary action if you have ever used an oil lamp. When a wick is placed in the oil, the oil travels up the wick to the top, where it will burn and give off light. As the oil at the lighted end evaporates and burns, it is replaced by more oil moving up the wick through capillary action.

With adult supervision, use a sharp knife to cut across the bottom of a stalk of celery. Examine the stalk carefully. You will see an interior of pith, or spongy tissue, containing scattered hollow tubes. You can carry out a simple experiment to see how these tubes work.

Take three clean drinking glasses. Pour a cup of water in each. Add three tablespoons of salt to one glass. Stir thoroughly to dissolve the salt. Put a piece of masking tape marked SALT on the glass. Use a clean spoon to measure three tablespoons of sugar in another glass. Stir the sugar solution thoroughly. Put a piece of tape marked SUGAR on that glass. Leave the third glass of water plain.

With adult supervision, cut off the bottom of three stalks of celery that have leaves on top, and put a stalk in each drinking glass. After three days, taste a leaf from each stalk. Do the three leaves taste differently from one another? Is one sweet? Is one salty? What does this taste test reveal about what is happening in the plant?

Put a piece of tape in the middle of each of three plates. Label one PLAIN, one SUGAR, and one SALT. Cut the stalk of celery that was in saltwater above the liquid line. Cut that top section in pieces and put it on the plate marked SALT. Do the same for the stalk that was in sugar water, but put it on the plate marked SUGAR. Do the same with the stalk that was in

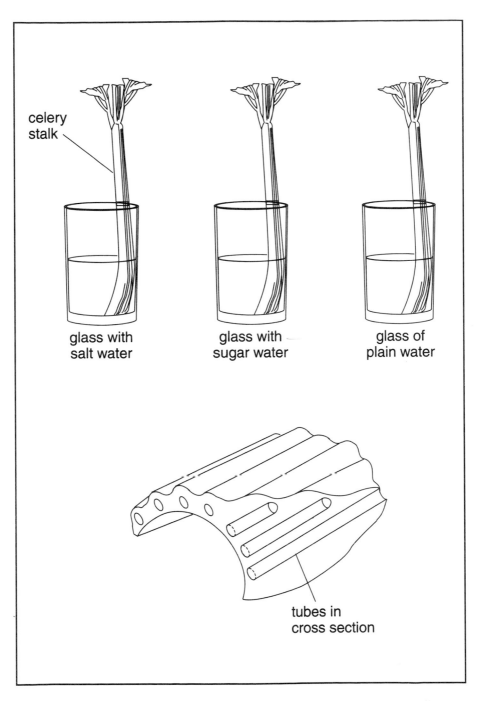

celery stalk

glass with salt water

glass with sugar water

glass of plain water

tubes in cross section

Observe the movement of water in vascular plants by studying stalks of celery.

plain water. Have several people sample the celery pieces and note whether they taste sweet, salty, or plain.

Further Explorations

Try to devise other experiments showing how water circulates in plants. Would the red food coloring travel faster or slower through a carnation if you used warm rather than cool water? What would happen with ice water?

Investigation 3

Will similar plants graft together?

Materials

* 2 small column-type cacti

* heavy gardening gloves

* 4 feet of thick yarn

* sharp knife

* rubbing alcohol

* old newspaper or two-foot-square piece of bubble wrap

* cotton balls

* notebook and pen

Grafting occurs when you insert a plant shoot with one or more buds into the stem, root, or branch of another plant so that you get a permanent union. Horticulturists practice grafting to create such things as combination trees with altered size and fruits. Grafting can be done with cactus plants.

Cacti are more than just sharp, prickly plants. The fruits of the giant saguaro cactus and the prickly pear cactus, for example, provide food for people and animals. Cactus flowers attract pollinators such as butterflies, bees, ants, and even nectar-feeding bats. Pollen from one part of a plant rubs off on the pollinator and is transferred to another part of the plant as the pollinator moves from blossom to blossom.

The body of the cactus is referred to as the corpus. It is a succulent stem containing the vascular bundle, or group of vessels. Around the bundle is a layer of tissue that is able to store water. Because few cacti have leaves, the corpus takes over the process of transpiration, or passing water vapor from the surface of the green plant tissue. To prevent loss of water during dry periods, the outer skin has only a few pores, called stomata.

Cactus plants will produce new cells that will join, or graft, with the cells of another cactus. To complete your grafting experiment, you will need two cacti that are unbranched and shaped like columns. The plants should have about the same circumference. If possible, choose two that are in square, plastic pots as deep as they are wide. These nonporous containers will prevent moisture loss. **Ask an adult for help** with this experiment and be very careful in handling cacti so that you do not get stuck with spines. Wearing heavy gardening gloves will help protect your hands.

Put the two cactus plants side by side. Lay out a two-foot piece of thick yarn underneath each of the potted plants. **With**

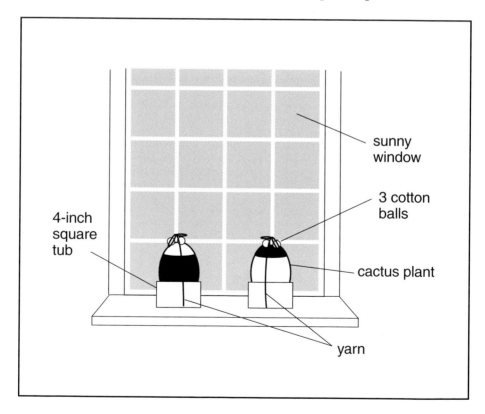

You can graft two cacti.

adult supervision, dip a sharp knife into rubbing alcohol to sterilize it. Fold a piece of newspaper into a thick pad or use a thick layer of bubble wrap. Wearing heavy gardening gloves and using the pad of paper or bubble wrap to protect your hands, slice off the top of each cactus plant about two inches from the top. Do not touch the cut surfaces of the plants. Keep them clean and free of germs and dirt.

While still wearing your gardening gloves and using a thick pad of paper or bubble wrap to protect your hands, switch the tops of the plants. Press each of the tops firmly into place. Put two or three cotton balls on top of each of the cactus plants. Pull the yarn up over the top of each plant over the protective cotton balls and tie securely.

Put the plants in a sunny spot and water once a week. Observe often. Note the time and date of each observation as well as what you see. After four to six weeks, the grafts should heal and you will be able to remove the yarn and cotton balls from the two cactus plants.

Do both of the plants survive? In time, do they flower? In what ways do they resemble each other?

Further Explorations

Consult with a local horticulturist, and with help, try grafting two other types of plants.

Investigation 4

What colors can you see in leaves?

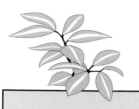

Leaves have tiny holes, called stomata, on their surfaces. When the leaves become warm, tiny drops of water escape through the stomata into the air as water vapor. This process is called transpiration.

Many trees shed their leaves in the fall in order to avoid water loss throughout the winter. As autumn approaches, trees stop producing chlorophyll, which is a green substance that is used in the chemical reaction that enables plants to make food. At this time of year, when the green pigment fades, other colors in the leaf can be seen.

You can find these other colors in leaves before autumn approaches. Take fresh beet leaves. These can come from a home garden, or you may be able to buy a bunch of beets with the leaves still attached. You may need to ask the produce manager of the grocery store for help, because sometimes clerks remove the leaves before putting the beets out for sale.

Tear four or five beet leaves into small pieces and put them in an old pie pan. When you have a pile of torn pieces of leaves, add a small quantity (about one tablespoonful) of white sand for grit. Add about two tablespoons of rubbing alcohol.

Using a rock, grind up the leaves. (If available, you can use a mortar and pestle.)

Continue grinding the leaves together with the rubbing alcohol and sand until you have ground them into a dark green liquid. Use a cotton swab to paint a spot of this dark green liquid on a white coffee filter cone, about halfway up the side of the filter. Put on two dozen coats of the green liquid, letting the spot dry between each coat.

Put about an inch of rubbing alcohol into a narrow glass jar. Place the coffee filter into the jar and submerge the tip in the rubbing alcohol. Be sure that the alcohol is not deep enough to reach the spot that you have painted on the side of

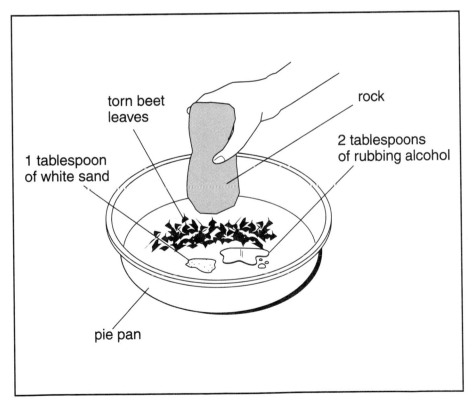

torn beet leaves

rock

2 tablespoons of rubbing alcohol

1 tablespoon of white sand

pie pan

By grinding leaves, you can search for hidden colors.

the filter. After ten minutes, remove the cone from the jar and spread it out on the table.

What colors do you see? Note the time, date, and species of leaf along with your observations in your science notebook.

Chromatography describes methods used to separate and identify mixtures of chemical compounds. This experiment makes use of paper chromatography. The paper cone has absorbed a small amount of water from the air. The colored chemicals from the ground leaves are dissolved by the alcohol and carried in the alcohol up through the cone. Some of the chemicals are much more soluble in the water in the paper cone than others. They stay put while the chemicals less soluble in water and more soluble in alcohol move on with the alcohol. As different-colored chemicals are left behind, colored bands are produced.

Further Explorations

What other experiments could you try? Repeat this experiment by using different kinds of leaves or using leaves that you collect at a different time of year. What results would you get by using spinach leaves? Record your observations, including the time, date, the type of leaf, and the colors you see.

Investigation 5

Will the use of fertilizer help produce more flowers on African violets and geraniums?

Materials

* * a flower of any type
* * poster board
* * soft drawing pencil
* * 2 potted African violets
* * 2 potted geraniums
* * masking tape
* * centimeter ruler
* * notebook and pen
* * water
* * water-soluble plant food
* * empty plastic milk jug

There are about two hundred thousand flowering species of plants. Although they differ in size and shape, they have the same basic parts. Roots anchor the plants and contain tubes, called xylem, that carry food substances and water up and down. Leaves, or modified stems acting as leaves, catch the sun. The sun acts on the chlorophyll to turn carbon dioxide and water into the sugars, starches, and oils that nourish the plant and, in turn, the animals that eat the plant. Flowers are the reproductive organs, containing male and female structures.

Examine a flower carefully. Although there are differences, flowers will have some things in common. Draw your flower on poster board and label its parts. The drawing on page 26 may be of help.

A typical flower has four sets of parts. The central pistil is surrounded by a ring of stamens, a ring of petals, and on the outside, a ring of sepals. The group of petals is called the corolla. The corolla attracts bees, butterflies, and birds, all of

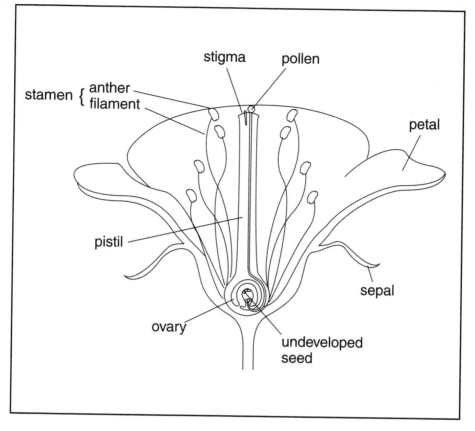

The basic parts of a flower

which help in plant pollination. The sepals form the calyx, which is usually green and protects the unopened bud.

Pollen is produced in the male parts of the flower, the stamens. The pistil and its appendages in the center are the female parts. They contain future fruits and seeds. Petals and sepals protect and support the flower's reproductive parts. When pollen is carried to a flower with female reproductive parts, pollen grains join with female cells inside the ovary, and seeds begin to form. These seeds can then grow into new plants.

Take two African violet plants of similar size. Use masking tape to label one pot WATER ONLY and the other pot PLANT FOOD ADDED. Keep the violets side by side where they receive some sunlight.

Take two potted geraniums of similar size. Use masking tape to label one pot WATER ONLY and the other pot PLANT FOOD ADDED. Keep the two geraniums right next to the African violets.

Take a careful measurement of the height and breadth of your plants and record this information in a notebook.

Follow the directions on a container of water-soluble plant food and mix the appropriate amount into a quart of water. Keep the solution in an empty plastic milk jug labeled PLANT FOOD. Water each of the plants about twice a week—when the soil feels dry to the touch—according to their labels. Water all the plants, using the same amount of water each time with each plant. Use only tap water when you water the potted plants labeled WATER ONLY.

As you water and fertilize your African violet and geranium, you cannot see anything happening. But remember that a flowering plant is busy night and day. During the daylight hours, the leaves of the plant are collecting the sun's energy. When it is dark, the plant uses this energy to create food in the form of sugars. Twenty-four hours a day, the plant's respiration is occurring.

Each week, note the plant growth, entering the time, date, and your observations in your notebook. Count the number of leaves and the number of blossoms. Does one African violet or geranium have larger leaves than the other? Are the leaves of one African violet or geranium a darker green than the other? Because they have received additional nourishment, the African violet and the geranium plants receiving plant food should be larger after a few months and have many more flowers than the plants receiving only water.

Further Explorations

What else might hinder or stimulate the growth of plants? If you used salt water on one set of plants, what effect would it have? You could use a water test kit and test the leachate (the liquid leaving the bottom of the pot) from each of the pots of soil for the presence of nitrate and phosphate. Are there differences?

Investigation 6

Are there ways to make seeds germinate faster?

Materials

* sponge
* small bowl and large bowl
* water
* handful of bird seed
* 12 pumpkin seeds
* two cups
* tea
* 3 clay pots
* potting soil
* masking tape
* notebook and pen

Seeds have protective outside coverings called seed coats. These seed coats must be opened to allow the tiny plant inside to grow. Acids or water will degrade or soften a seed coat and allow the seed to sprout. Some seeds get swallowed by animals and are exposed to stomach acids. Some land in soil and are exposed to soil acids such as tannin. Acids degrade the seed coats. Others fall into shallow streams. Water softens the seed coats.

To sprout, many seeds need only water. Cut a sponge in half and place it in a small bowl. Pour water over the sponge into the bowl to a level of about one-quarter inch. Take a small handful of birdseed and sprinkle the seeds on top of the sponge. Using a large glass bowl, cover the smaller bowl containing the sponge, water, and seeds.

When the seeds sprout, take off the large bowl and place the small bowl in a sunny spot. Add water as needed to keep the sponge wet at all times. The water the seed coats received from the sponge will have softened them and allowed them to sprout.

Does softening of the seed coat speed the growth of the seeds?

Soak four pumpkin seeds in a cup of water and four other pumpkin seeds in a cup of tea at room temperature. (The tea contains tannic acid.) Leave four pumpkin seeds dry. After twenty-four hours, plant the pumpkin seeds in clay pots containing potting soil, following the directions on the pumpkin seed packet. Place the four pumpkin seeds that had been soaked in water in one pot. Use a pen and a piece of masking tape to label that pot SOAKED IN WATER.

Place the four pumpkins seeds that had been soaked in tea in a second pot. Label that pot SOAKED IN TEA.

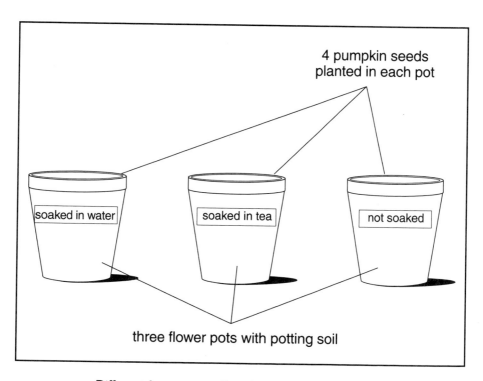

Different factors may affect the speed of germination.

Plant the four dry pumpkin seeds in a third pot. Label that pot NOT SOAKED.

Put the pots in a sunny spot and water the plants when the soil feels dry. Check the plants every day. When do they sprout? How many sprout?

Keep a record of your observations, noting the time and date and what you see each time. Did soaking the seeds have any effect? Was there a difference between seeds soaked in water and those soaked in tea? After several weeks, was there any difference in the size of the young plants?

Further Explorations

In what other ways might you affect the speed at which seeds germinate? Would the temperature of the spot where you placed the pots affect the speed of germination? If you soaked some seeds for twenty-four hours and other seeds for forty-eight hours, would the difference in soaking time affect the speed of germination? Do different species of seeds have different germination times?

Investigation 7

Will peanut plants grow if they lose their seed leaves?

Materials

* 10 unsalted, raw peanuts in their shells

* microscope

* jar with lid

* water

* 3 paper towels

* baking pan

* clear plastic wrap

* notebook and pen

* 6 paper cups

* potting soil

* scissors

* masking tape

* ruler

Seeds come in many sizes and shapes. Some, like poppy seeds, are small; others, like avocado pits, are large. The coconut is an even larger seed. Peanuts are also seeds. You can do an interesting experiment by using eight peanuts. First, you need to buy some unsalted raw peanuts in their shells. You can find these at organic produce and health food stores. (Be sure you are not buying salted, roasted peanuts.)

Take off the peanut shell from one of the peanuts. Carefully split each of the nuts in half. At one end of each nut, you will see a bump. This is a baby plant. If you carefully remove the bump and place it under a microscope, you might be able to see some tiny leaves.

Take the shells off the other nine peanuts and place the nuts in a jar. Add enough water to cover the peanuts and put the cover on the jar. Let it stand overnight. The next day you will see that the peanuts are larger than they were before. Water has soaked into them and caused them to swell. The water has

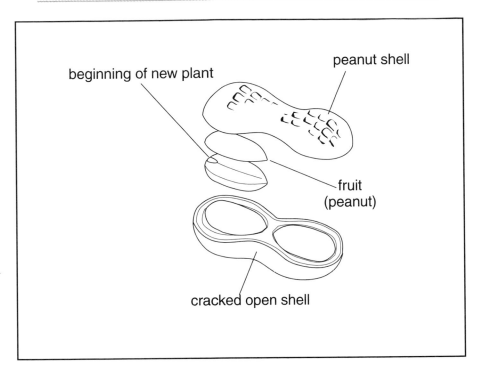

Examine a new peanut plant.

softened the stored food in the peanuts and dissolved some of it. The peanuts can now use this food to grow.

Soak several thick paper towels in water. Use these wet towels to line a baking pan. Put all the peanuts that you have soaked overnight on the wet towels. Then cover the pan with a piece of clear plastic wrap.

Place the pan in a sunny spot. Observe what happens. In your science notebook, write down the date and time of your observations and what you observe. If the paper towels begin to dry out, add more water. Do not let the towels become dry.

In about three days, you will notice that your peanuts have turned green. The halves will have opened out. These green halves are called cotyledons. These seed leaves contain stored food. Peanut seedlings will begin to grow.

During the process of germination, an underground seed absorbs water. Once the softened seed coat splits, the beginning of the root system grows downward. Soon after, a shoot appears. At first it is bent, and its tip is buried in the seed leaves. The shoot grows long and exerts enough pressure to break through the surface of the soil. Once it is above ground, it straightens, grows toward the light, and the first true leaves appear.

Fill six paper cups with potting soil. Choose six healthy-looking seedlings that are starting to grow leaves at one end and roots at the other.

For one seedling, use scissors to snip off both of the seed leaves. Then plant the seedling in a cup with the root pointing down. Use a piece of masking tape to label this cup A: NO SEED LEAVES. Do exactly the same thing to another seedling and plant it in a cup labeled B: NO SEED LEAVES.

Choose another two peanut seedlings. Snip off only one of the seed leaves from each seedling. Plant each in a cup with the root pointing down. Use masking tape to label these cups C: ONE SEED LEAF and D: ONE SEED LEAF.

Choose two more peanut seedlings. Leave both of the seed leaves on, and plant each of these, root down, in cups labeled E: BOTH SEED LEAVES and F: BOTH SEED LEAVES.

Place the six cups in a sunny spot and water them when the soil feels dry. Check the cups twice a day for two weeks. Record in your science notebook the time and date of each observation and note what you see. Measure the height of the seedlings from the soil to the top of the plant. Count the number of leaves.

At the end of the two weeks, are the plants in cups A and B as tall and as full as the plants in cups E and F? Are the plants in cups C and D as tall and as full as plants E and F? Was there a time during the two weeks when one or more of the plants were noticeably taller and fuller than any of the others?

Further Explorations

What else might affect the peanut seedlings? If you did not cut off the seed leaves but covered them in foil, what effect might this have on the young plant?

Investigation 8

What happens to seeds in a microwave oven?

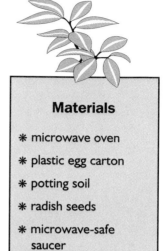

Materials

* microwave oven
* plastic egg carton
* potting soil
* radish seeds
* microwave-safe saucer
* water
* notebook and pen

Microwave ovens use electromagnetic waves to heat food. In this process, the waves excite molecules in the food, producing heat. In this experiment, the microwave will be a convenient and quick way of showing the effect of heat on seeds.

Prepare a plastic egg carton for planting by marking the pairs of egg cups 0, 5, 10, 20, 40, and 60. Fill each cup with potting soil in which you will plant radish seeds.

One seed will be planted in each cup marked 0, indicating that these seeds had no exposure in a microwave.

Place two seeds on a microwave-safe saucer in the microwave oven; heat them for five seconds at a HIGH power setting. Take them out and plant these two seeds in the cups marked 5.

Continue with this process, planting two seeds exposed in the microwave oven for twenty seconds in the cups marked 20; two seeds that were exposed in the microwave oven for forty seconds in the cups marked 40, and two seeds that were exposed in the microwave oven for sixty seconds in the cups marked 60.

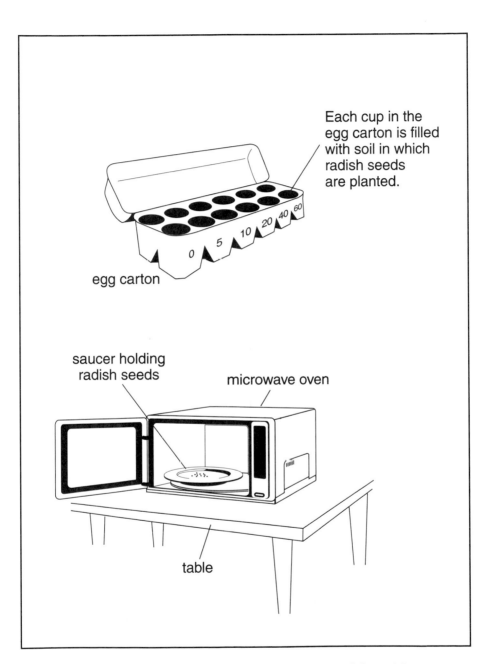

Each cup in the egg carton is filled with soil in which radish seeds are planted.

egg carton

saucer holding radish seeds

microwave oven

table

What is the effect of microwave exposure on radish seeds?

After all the seeds have been planted in the appropriate cups, gently pour water onto the soil. Place the egg-carton garden in a sunny window. When the soil feels dry, water each of the egg carton sections equally.

Check your egg-carton garden daily. In your science notebook, note the time and date of each observation and what you saw. Which seeds sprout?

Further Explorations

Read and learn more about microwaves. Consider what other experiments in botany might make use of a microwave oven. What, for example, would happen to a young, healthy plant that was placed in a microwave oven for a few seconds? Would a few seconds in a microwave cause a pine cone to release its seeds? Be sure to do any experiments of your own design under adult supervision.

Part II

Environmental Needs

The experiments in Part I were designed to reveal the structure and function of roots, leaves, stems, flowers, and seeds. This next section examines the environmental needs of plants with respect to water, temperature, light, and air quality.

To grow well in homes, gardens, and in the wild, plants must have the right conditions, including the right amount of water. Some plants thrive in dry areas while others need wet ground.

The soil must be free of harmful chemicals that can soak into the water table and enter plants through their roots.

Plants also need clean air. Home, cars, and factories burn fossil fuels that can pollute the air with gases. These gases rise, mix with water, and produce sulfuric and nitric acids. Plants may be killed when these chemicals fall as acid rain.

Investigation 9

How do plants respond to air pollution?

Lichens are unique in that they are a combination of plants from two different groups. The plants that unite to produce lichen are an alga and a fungus. The alga manufactures food and the fungus absorbs water from the atmosphere. In this way, each part provides what the other needs. There is also an exchange of organic compounds between the components.

Plants photosynthesize by taking in carbon dioxide. In many parts of the world there is air pollution from factory smoke, wood-burning stoves, and automobile exhaust. Stomata, the small openings on the underside of leaves, take in whatever is in the air. If there is a lot of smoke in the air, the stomata take in pollution as well as carbon dioxide.

How do lichens respond to air pollution? Find several lichens growing on rocks or fallen tree limbs. Lichens may appear orange, yellow, or gray-green. Pictures of them are available in encyclopedias and plant books. Lichens are found on rocks that have been left undisturbed for many years. The rocks need to be exposed to sunlight and water but do not need to be located by streams or lakes. Sometimes these rocks

Materials

* lichens growing on small rocks or fallen tree limbs
* 3 clear plastic bags
* baking pan
* atomizer
* water
* candle or splint of wood
* match
* twist tie
* notebook and pen

are collected and brought to gardens because they are decorative. With permission from a property owner, you can collect two small lichen-covered rocks for use in this experiment.

Remove two small rocks or small pieces of fallen tree limbs on which lichens are growing. Be sure to take only the two small specimens you need for your experiment. Put each specimen in a clear plastic bag and set each bag in a baking pan outdoors in a sunny spot. Open the bags and spray the lichens with water each day to keep them moist.

With adult supervision, light a candle or small splint of wood. Blow it out. Quickly collect the smoke from the candle or splint in a third plastic bag. Seal the bag to prevent the

Expose lichens to air pollution.

smoke from escaping. Carry the bag outdoors, and put one lichen specimen inside the bag of smoke. Seal it with a twist tie. Leave it in the smoke for two hours. Then take the rock or limb out and put it back in its clean plastic bag in the baking pan.

Repeat this process, collecting a new bag of smoke each day and always putting the same specimen in the bag of smoke.

Each day when you spray water on both specimens examine them. In your notebook, record the time and date and any changes you observe.

After six weeks, examine the two lichen-covered rocks or lichen-covered branches for a final time. Is there any difference between your control plant, which you simply sprayed with water daily and kept in a sunny place outdoors, and the lichen-covered rock or branch that was placed in smoke for two hours a day?

Further Explorations

Pollutants have effects on plants other than lichens. Try repeating your experiment with other seedlings or small plants. Are the results similar? Are some varieties of plants hardier than others?

Investigation 10

How much water do seeds need to sprout?

Materials

* 2 plastic egg cartons
* potting soil
* marking pen
* 24 dried lima beans
* eyedropper
* notebook and pen

A seed must break through its hard protective coat in order for the plant to grow. If you performed Investigation 7 in this book, you learned about ways to speed the germination of seeds. You found that soaking seeds overnight in water or tea is one way to soften the seed coat.

What is the optimum amount of water required to encourage newly planted dry seeds to germinate and grow?

Fill each of the cups of two plastic egg cartons with rich potting soil. On both cartons, use a marking pen and number each cup 1 through 12. Mark the cover of one carton COVER KEPT OPEN. Mark the cover of the other carton COVER KEPT CLOSED.

Plant a dry bean seed in each of the twenty-four egg pockets. Place both egg cartons side by side in a warm place. At twelve-hour cycles, such as each morning at 8:00 A.M. and each evening at 8:00 P.M., add drops of water to your beans by using an eyedropper. Put only one drop in the cup marked 1, put two drops in the cup marked 2, put three drops in the cup marked 3, and so on. After you have watered all the plants, close the cover on the carton marked COVER KEPT CLOSED. (By

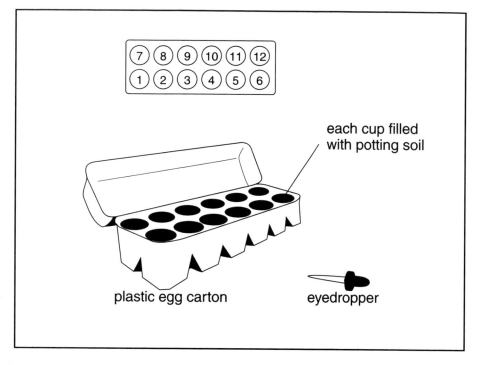

What is the optimal amount of water needed for sprouting lima beans?

closing this cover, you will help keep the moisture in.) Leave the cover open on the carton marked COVER KEPT OPEN.

Each morning after you add the water drops, record your observations, including the date and time, in your science notebook. If you live in an area with high humidity, your results may differ from someone who lives in a dry area.

Continue watering for a month. When the beans have sprouted, move the egg cartons to a sunny spot and leave both egg carton covers open. Continue to water as before.

What do you observe? Does there seem to be an optimal amount of water for seed germination? Can you give a plant too much water?

Further Explorations

Repeat this experiment by using different seeds, some for vegetables and some for flowers. Does the optimal amount of water vary with the type of seed?

Investigation 11

Will seeds sprout in a refrigerator?

Seeds sprout when they have the right amount of warmth, water, and sometimes light. Will cold temperatures slow or speed germination? Is there a particular temperature that is optimal for the germination of seeds?

To begin, soak eight dried bean seeds overnight in a glass of water.

Materials

* drinking glass
* water
* 8 dried bean seeds
* 2 pie pans
* paper towels
* refrigerator
* notebook and pen

The next morning, place four of the beans in a metal pie pan on top of sheets of wet paper towels. Store this tray in a warm, dark closet. Place the other four beans in a pie pan on top of sheets of wet paper towels and put them in the refrigerator. (Be sure to tell your family about these pans so that they do not accidentally disrupt your experiment.)

Each day, examine the seeds. Add water if the paper towels start to dry. In your notebook, record the time, date, and what you observe.

After two weeks, take the seeds that have been stored in the refrigerator and move them next to the beans in the closet. Continue to keep the paper towels moist. Check the seeds each day and record the time, date, and any changes you observe.

What do you observe in the second two weeks? Did the seeds you stored in the refrigerator sprout in the refrigerator? Did they sprout after you moved them out of the refrigerator?

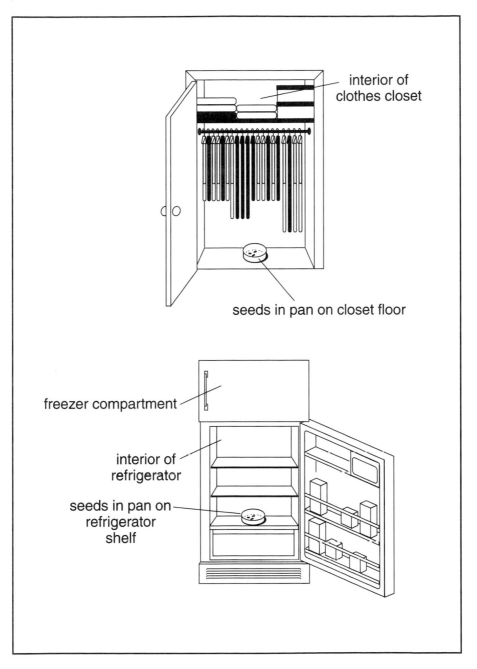

interior of
clothes closet

seeds in pan on closet floor

freezer compartment

interior of
refrigerator

seeds in pan on
refrigerator
shelf

Will cold temperature prevent seeds from sprouting?

Further Explorations

Do you think what you learned about temperature and bean seeds would be true for other seeds? What would happen if you used flower seeds? If you kept seeds in the refrigerator for a month or more, would they sprout when you moved them out of the refrigerator?

Investigation 12

How does sunlight affect plant growth?

Usually when you think of starting new plants, you think of planting seeds. But there are other ways to raise plants. One way is to grow a plant from its root. Sweet potatoes are roots that have lots of food stored in them. Under the right conditions, this stored food will help a new plant grow.

With the right sweet potato and some patience, you can grow a very beautiful vine. First, try to find sweet potatoes that show some signs of life. Look for little purple bumps at one end of the potato. (White potatoes will work, too, but they do not grow into as attractive a plant.)

Fill four tall jars about an inch from the top with water. Put a sweet potato onto each jar, with the narrow end in the water. If your jar has a narrow neck, push the potato down into the jar so that at least a third of it is in the water. If you have a widemouthed jar, stick three toothpicks into the potato, equidistant in a circle around the middle of the potato, and hang the potato on the jar from the toothpicks. Put a piece of masking tape on each jar. Label the jars A, B, C, and D.

Put all four jars in a warm, dark spot. Every few days, check the potatoes. In your science notebook, record the time, date, and anything you observe happening to the potatoes.

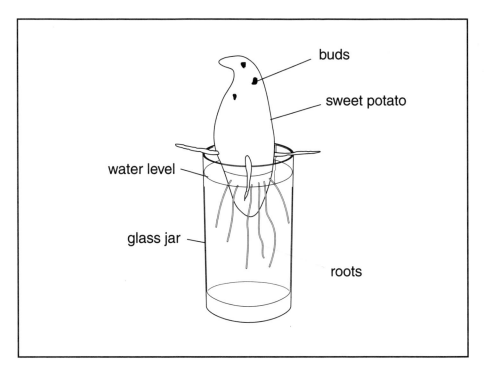

Grow a sweet potato in water.

After several weeks, when the potatoes sprout and begin to grow roots, move plants A and B to a sunny window, and leave plants C and D in the closet.

Continue to monitor both sets of potatoes, always entering the time and date of your observations and the changes that you see in your science notebook. Add fresh water as needed.

After two of the growing plants have been kept in the sunlight for two weeks, measure the sprouts of all four plants, recording the time, date, and number and length of the sprouts.

Then switch the jars—place plants C and D in the sunny window and move A and B into the closet. Be sure to enter the time and date of this switch in your science notebook. Leave the plants in their new positions for two weeks. Continue to monitor growth and record your observations in the notebook. Also check the color of the sprouts and leaves. Continue to add water to each of the jars as needed.

Finally, put all four plants in the sunny window for two weeks. At the end of this time, examine all four plants carefully. Record your observations. Count the number of sprouts and measure their height. Note the color of the leaves. Can you see any differences between plants A and B and plants C and D? Did keeping plants in the sunlight make a difference in their growth?

Further Explorations

Cut one of the potatoes into several pieces, being sure that a sprout is growing from each piece. If you put the pieces in additional jars of water, will each sprout continue to grow? If you tried this experiment with a sweet potato, you might want to repeat it, using a white potato, and record the differences in the two varieties.

Investigation 13

What does yeast do?

There are hundreds of varieties of yeast. A characteristic of many yeasts is their ability to convert sugar into carbon dioxide and alcohol. Brewer's yeast is used in making beer, wine, ale, and bread.

If you have ever made yeast bread or watched others make it, you know that after the dough is mixed, it is left to stand for a time before it is baked. As the dough stands, it rises, becoming almost twice as large as it was before. After it rises, the bread is baked. The baked bread is light because it has tiny air holes in it.

What makes the bread rise? The bread rises because of microscopic fungi. These tiny organisms are called yeasts, and they are similar to molds and mushrooms. Like other fungi, yeasts cannot make their own food, and they are not green.

Yeast grows when it has sugar and water. As it grows, a bud appears at its end. When it is big enough, it sends out another bud. This growth continues until there are many new yeast cells.

Materials

* 2 large bowls
* warm water
* 3 tablespoons of sugar
* 1 tablespoon salt
* 2 tablespoons of shortening, softened
* about 8 cups flour
* wooden spoon
* margarine
* 2 clean cloths
* package of dry, granular yeast
* notebook and pen
* two bread pans, 9" x 5" x 3"
* oven
* oven mitts
* wire racks
* centimeter ruler
* bread board and knife

As yeast grows in the warm, moist bread dough, it gives off alcohol and carbon dioxide. The alcohol and carbon dioxide get trapped inside the dough. The carbon dioxide bubbles make the dough rise.

Once the bread is baked, the carbon dioxide bubbles escape and the alcohol evaporates. The heat kills the yeast. But left in the dough are the holes from the carbon dioxide bubbles. These holes make the bread light and airy.

The following activity will help you see the importance of yeast in bread making. Because you will be using an oven, **ask an adult** to help you. You will be making two loaves of white bread, only one of which will contain yeast.

First, wash your hands thoroughly. Mix together into one mixing bowl 1 1/8 cup of lukewarm water, 1 1/2 tablespoons sugar, and 1/2 tablespoon salt. Add 1 tablespoon soft shortening and 3 1/2 cups flour. Mix in the flour with a wooden spoon, and then mix by hand. When the dough begins to leave the sides of the bowl, place it onto a lightly floured board to knead.

Knead the dough by folding it toward you and then pressing down and away from you with the heel of your hand. Give the dough a quarter turn, and repeat. Continue kneading until the dough is smooth, elastic, and does not stick to the board. Grease a bowl with margarine. Put the dough in the bowl, and then turn it once so that the greased side is up. Cover with a damp cloth.

Prepare another batch of dough. Mix together in a mixing bowl 7/8 cups of lukewarm water, 1 1/2 tablespoons sugar, and 1/2 tablespoon salt. In a cup, mix together 1 package of dry granular yeast and 1/4 cup very warm water. Stir the yeast and

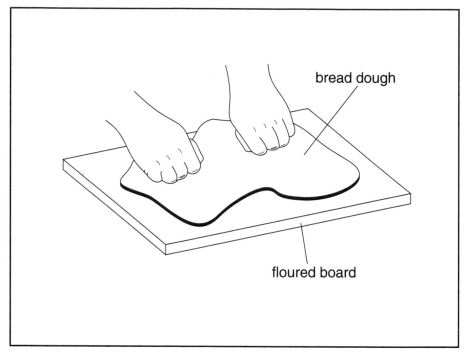

bread dough

floured board

Experiment with yeast.

water together thoroughly and then add it to your mixture. Next, add 1 tablespoon soft shortening and 3 1/2 cups of flour. Mix thoroughly first with a spoon and then by hand.

Knead as described earlier. Grease a bowl with margarine. Put the dough in the bowl, turning once so the greased side is up. Cover with a damp cloth.

Let the two bowls sit side by side in a warm, draft-free spot for two hours.

At the end of two hours check on both bowls of dough. Note the time and date, and write your observations in your notebook.

Thrust your fist into the middle of both bowls of dough. Pull the edges to the center and turn the dough completely over. Cover both bowls and place them in the same warm spot for another forty-five minutes.

Check the dough again, and record your observations in your notebook. Flatten each piece of dough into an oblong shape, about 15 inches by 5 inches and press out the air. Bring the ends to the center, overlap them, and seal by pressing down firmly. Place in greased loaf pans. Cover with a cloth, and wait another hour. **Under adult supervision**, bake both loaves of bread in a 425°F oven for 25 to 30 minutes or until brown. Using oven mitts, remove the loaves from the oven and let them cool in the pans for 10 minutes on wire racks. Again using the oven mitts, tap out the loaves and let them finish cooling on wire racks.

Compare the appearance of the two loaves of bread. Measure the height of the two loaves. **Ask an adult** to slice the bread. Notice the difference in texture. Does one loaf of bread have little holes in it? Compare the taste of the two loaves. Record all your observations in your notebook.

Further Explorations

Think of other experiments that might involve yeast. For example, what might happen if you took a cake of yeast and put it in a microwave for ten seconds before using it in a bread recipe? What would happen if, in your bread recipe, you substituted boiling water or ice water for warm water? When using an oven or stove, be sure to work under adult supervision.

Investigation 14

What speeds the growth of mold?

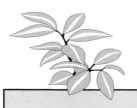

Fungi such as molds, mildews, and mushrooms lack chlorophyll. They reproduce by means of asexual spores, which are primitive reproductive bodies. Fungi give off spores that make their way into the air, water, and soil. Lacking chlorophyll, the green pigment that helps plants make their food, fungi have other means of survival. They live by feeding on other living things and on decaying matter. The following experiment will help you learn more about molds. (*If you are allergic to molds, it would be wise to skip this experiment.*)

For this project, use the bread you baked from Investigation 13, bake a new loaf of bread, or choose a store-bought loaf that contains no preservatives. Mold inhibitors are contained in many commercial bread products to prevent or reduce the growth of mold, which would spoil this experiment.

Materials

* slice of bread without preservatives
* water
* plastic sandwich bags
* twist ties
* notebook and pen
* knife
* carrot
* tomato
* broccoli
* sweet potato
* 2 cups
* plastic sandwich bags
* 2 tablespoons sugar
* cotton swabs
* masking tape
* tablespoon
* 2 shoe boxes with lids
* 6 small jars with lids
* slices of potato
* shredded wheat biscuit
* 2 small pieces of cake
* refrigerator
* dust mask (optional)

Sprinkle water on a piece of bread, place it in a plastic bag, close the bag with a twist tie, and put the bag in a dark, warm spot for several days. Wait until you have a noticeable crop of mold on the bread. In your notebook, record the color of the mold and what fraction of the bread is covered in the mold. Then, **with adult supervision**, use a knife to cut two slices each of carrot, tomato, broccoli, and sweet potato.

Set aside one cup of plain water and a second cup of water into which you have stirred and dissolved two tablespoons of sugar.

Dip a cotton swab into the mold on the bread and paint the mold on one slice of tomato. Put a piece of masking tape on a plastic bag and label it PLAIN WATER. Put the tomato into a plastic bag, sprinkle it with two tablespoons of plain water, and close the bag with a twist tie. Throw away the cotton swab.

With a fresh cotton swab, paint mold on the second slice of tomato. Put a piece of masking tape on a plastic bag and label it SUGAR WATER. Sprinkle the second slice of tomato with sugar water, put it in a bag, and secure it with a twist tie.

Repeat the process with the slices of carrot, sweet potato, and broccoli. Use a clean cotton swab each time you dip into the mold. Keep the bag of moldy bread for future use.

Place the four bags containing the vegetables swabbed with mold and sprinkled with plain water in a shoe box and close the lid. Label the box PLAIN WATER.

Put the four bags containing the vegetables swabbed with mold and sprinkled with sugar water in another shoe box and close the lid. Label this box SUGAR WATER. Put the boxes in a warm, dark spot.

Check the boxes in four days. Record the time, date, and your observations in your science notebook. Did more mold grow in one box than the other? Did adding sugar speed the growth of mold? Is all the mold the same color? Is it the same color as the original bread mold?

Using the piece of bread on which you started the crop of mold, try another experiment. Put a small piece of masking tape on each of six small jars. Pour one tablespoon of water into each of six jars. Dip a cotton swab into the bread mold and use it to rub the mold onto two slices of potato. Take a clean swab and use it to rub mold onto both halves of a broken shredded wheat biscuit. Use another clean swab to put mold on two small pieces of cake.

Put each of the food samples into its own jar and close the lid. Use your pen to mark these jars for what they contain (potato, shredded wheat, or cake) and add C for closet or R for refrigerator.

Put the three jars marked with Cs into a shoe box. Put the lid on, and put the shoe box in a warm, dark closet.

Put the three jars marked with Rs into another shoe box. Put the lid on, and place the shoe box in the refrigerator.

Wash your hands thoroughly with soap and water after working with the food and mold. Remember that spores cause allergies in some people, so you should be careful in handling your moldy food. Be sure not to breathe in spores. You may even want to wear a dust mask.

Check often for growth of mold by looking into the three glass jars being kept in the closet and the jars in the refrigerator. Record the time and date of each observation as well as what you observe.

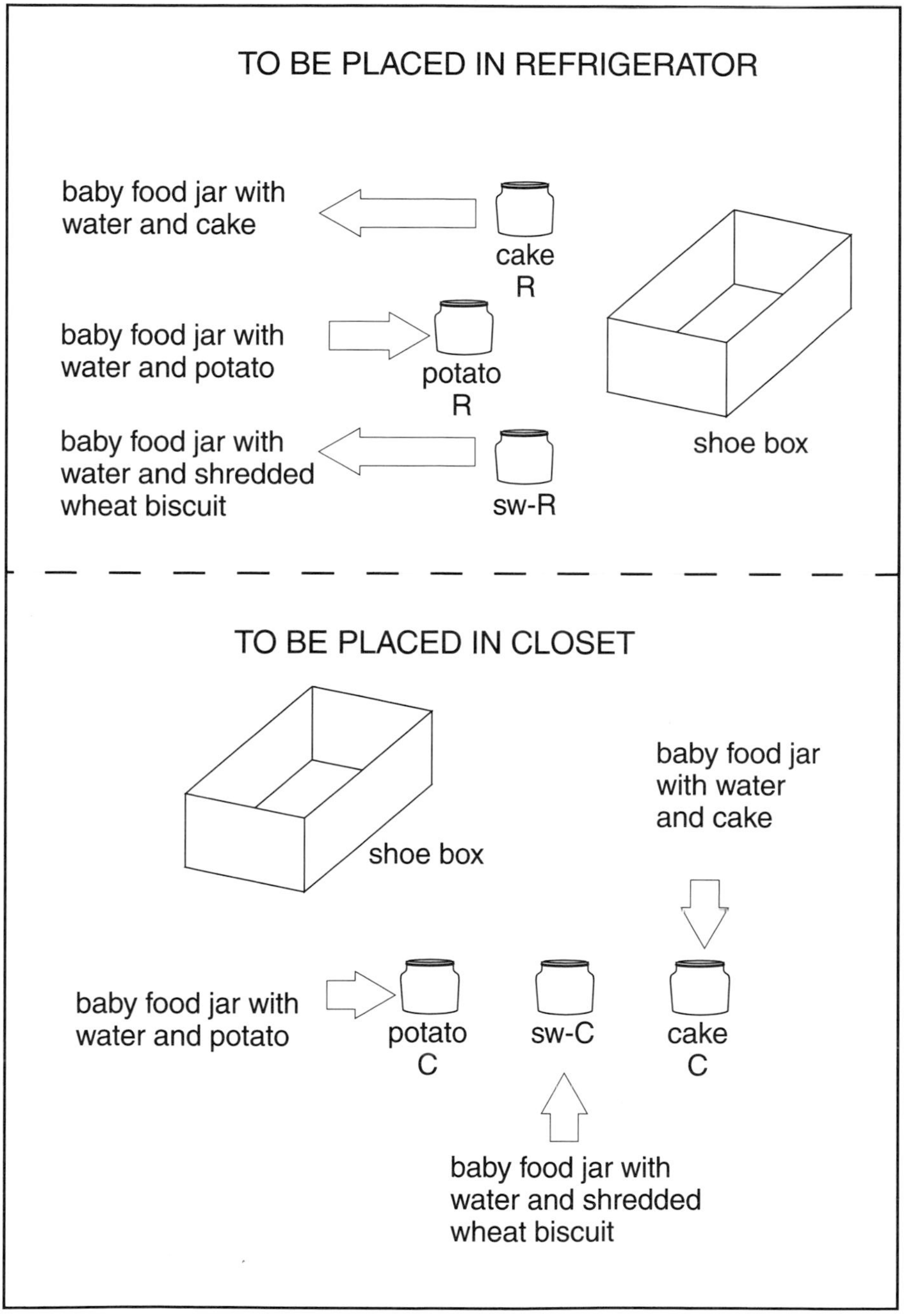

Study the growth of mold.

Did mold grow on the food in all six jars? In which jar did mold first appear? In which jar and on what food did mold grow the slowest? What colors of mold were produced?

Further Explorations

Mold grows on many kinds of food. You might want to try this experiment by using mold that has grown on an orange or on a piece of cheese. What would happen to food on which you have placed mold if it were kept in a sunny spot instead of in a closet or refrigerator?

Investigation 15

Is there an easy way to see spores?

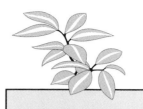

Fungi have no chlorophyll, so they cannot produce their own food. Like humans, they must get the nutrients they need from other organisms. The fungi that get their nourishment from dead organisms are called saprophytes.

Materials

∗ caps of several wild mushrooms

∗ sheets of white paper

∗ sheets of black paper

∗ 2 widemouthed jars

∗ notebook and pen

Mushrooms belong to the group of plants called fungi. They are found in meadows, woodlands, and pastures in temperate and tropical climates when the weather is moist and warm. Wild mushrooms may grow on a decaying log or from a pile of dead leaves. There are mushrooms as small as your fingernail and others that are as large as basketballs.

The easiest mushroom for you to find may be the common meadow mushroom that is often seen in lawns and parks. It has a cap that grows on top of its stem in the summer.

Cut off the caps of two meadow mushrooms and look underneath carefully. You will see something like a bicycle wheel with many "spokes" running from the center to the outer edge. These are called the mushroom gills.

The gills of a mushroom are covered with spores. When they are ripe, the spores fall. Some are blown by the wind. An animal may brush against them and send spores traveling.

More than a billion spores may fall in a few days. Only a few will reach a place on the ground where they can grow.

You can make a spore print by putting one mushroom cap, gill side down, on top of a sheet of white paper. Put a second mushroom cap, gill side down, on top of a sheet of black paper. Put a widemouthed jar, such as a clean mayonnaise jar, over each mushroom cap. Leave these setups in a spot where they will not be disturbed for twenty-four hours, such as on top of a bookcase or on a coffee table.

After twenty-four hours, carefully remove the jar and then lift each mushroom cap straight up off the paper. Do not touch the paper. If you touch the spore print, it will smudge.

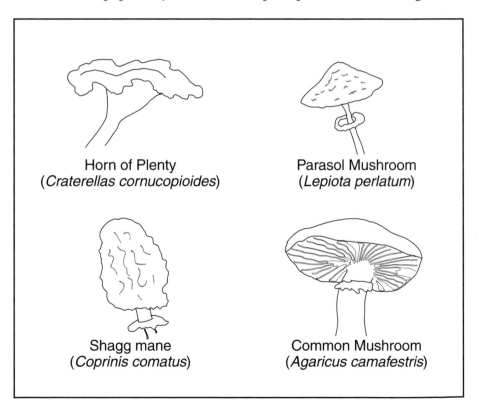

Horn of Plenty
(*Craterellas cornucopioides*)

Parasol Mushroom
(*Lepiota perlatum*)

Shagg mane
(*Coprinis comatus*)

Common Mushroom
(*Agaricus camafestris*)

Make spore prints from mushrooms.

The spores will have left a print of the gills. You can see them because hundreds of thousands of spores have dropped onto the paper. Since some spores are white or yellow, they will show up well on dark paper. Other spores are dark and will show up on white paper.

Write the time, date, and results of your attempt to make spore prints in your science notebook.

If you can hike in an area where there are different kinds of mushrooms, collect the caps of several. Always take two caps so that you can place one on light and one on dark paper. Do not take more than you are going to use. If you are on private property, be sure to ask for permission to hike there and to collect your mushroom caps.

You may find that some caps do not have gills. These mushrooms have small tubes through which the spores pass into the air or onto the ground. You can still make spore prints, but instead of having the pattern of the gills, you will have the pattern of the mushroom's tubes.

Remember, do not eat the mushrooms that you collect. Some mushrooms are poisonous, and only an expert can tell some varieties from others.

Further Explorations

If you are fortunate enough to live where commercial mushrooms are grown, you may be able to arrange for a field trip to learn how they are grown, harvested, and shipped for market. The produce manager at your local grocery store might be able to put you in touch with his mushroom supplier.

Part III

Life Processes

One of the critical things to remember if you decide to design a science fair project in botany is that many of these projects cannot be done hastily. Time is required to show the difference that variables make in plant growth.

When you vary the amount of sunlight or water that a plant receives, or when you add a fertilizer or a pollutant to the soil or air in which a plant is growing, it takes time for the effect on the plant to be noticeable.

This section deals with the life processes of plants. Activities include examining how leaves function with varying degrees of air and light; how roots grow and how they respond to different kinds of soils and to substances in soils; how plants reproduce from seeds, stems, leaves, and cuttings; and how plants respond to light.

Investigation 16

What happens when a leaf cannot photosynthesize?

Materials

* 4 healthy house plants such as philodendrons
* petroleum jelly
* masking tape
* water
* notebook and pen
* camera and film (optional)
* small, soft cloth

Green plants contain chlorophyll. Chlorophyll uses energy from sunlight to combine carbon dioxide from the air with water to make food for the plant. This complex process, called photosynthesis, usually takes place in a plant's leaves. Excess water and oxygen, by-products of photosynthesis, are released into the air.

Some plants are evergreens; others are deciduous: Their leaves will drop off during certain times of the year. On the underside of deciduous leaves are small openings, called stomata, that take in whatever is in the air. Plants take in carbon dioxide from the air and release water vapor through these stomata. The following experiment will show that if you block the stomata, the plant will not be able to photosynthesize.

Choose four healthy house plants of the same species that are approximately the same size with the same number of leaves. Philodendron will work well.

Thinly coat the underside of two leaves on one plant with petroleum jelly. This will prevent the stomata from receiving air. Put a piece of masking tape on this pot and mark it A: TWO LEAVES BLOCKED.

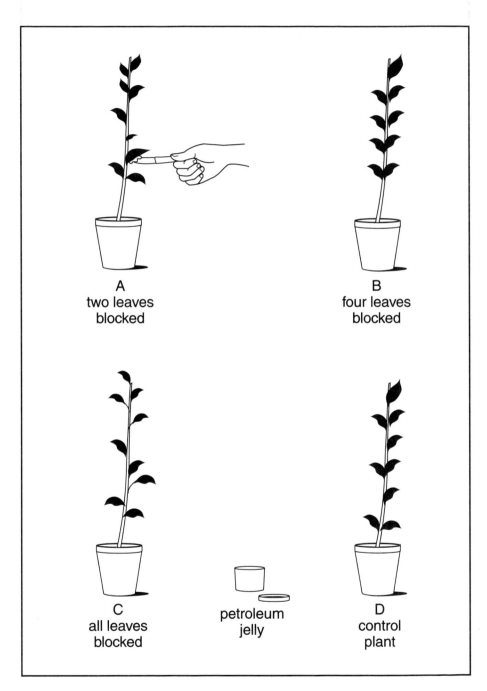

Show the effect of blocking the stomata on plant leaves.

Coat the undersides of four leaves on another plant. Put a piece of masking tape on this pot and mark it B: FOUR LEAVES BLOCKED.

Coat the undersides of all the leaves on a third plant with petroleum jelly. Put a piece of masking tape on this pot and mark it C: ALL LEAVES BLOCKED.

Do nothing to the fourth plant. Label the pot with a piece of masking tape marked D: CONTROL PLANT.

Keep all four plants side by side in a sunny spot. Give all the plants the same amount of water when the soil feels dry.

Record your observations for all four plants regularly, noting the time and date in your notebook. Examine the leaves that you covered with petroleum jelly. After several days, do all the leaves on all four plants look green and shiny? Do any curl and turn brown?

If a camera is available to you, this experiment lends itself well to taking close-up photographs showing the condition of the plant leaves. These photographs may be included in your science notebook. Be sure to note the time and date of each picture and show the identifying masking tape on each pot so that you will be certain which of the plants you are photographing.

After a week, use a soft cloth and warm water to remove all the petroleum jelly from the underside of the leaves of plant C. Wash each leaf thoroughly and gently.

Continue to observe all four plants, making regular notations in your notebook. Compare the growth, or lack of growth, between the control plant and the other plants. Note the number, condition, and color of the leaves.

Further Explorations

Try to think of other ways of blocking plant stomata. Would other leaves, such as geranium leaves, respond in the same way? If you have trees in your yard, would this experiment work on the leaves of those species?

Investigation 17

How do leaves affect plant growth?

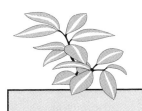

Materials

* 2 healthy house plants such as philodendrons

* black plastic, such as a garbage bag

* scissors

* masking tape

* water

* notebook and pen

The leaf is the part of a green plant that does the chemical work of photosynthesis. A green pigment called chlorophyll, which is present in all green growing things, captures the sunlight, which provides energy to make food for the plant. What happens when leaves are deprived of sunlight?

Take two healthy potted plants of the same species and approximately the same size. Each should have at least ten leaves. A philodendron is a good choice.

Use black plastic material, such as a piece of a garbage bag, for a covering. First, cut a square large enough to completely cover a leaf, top and bottom. Poke some thin holes in the plastic so that air can enter. Use masking tape to hold the plastic securely around the leaf. Repeat this process with two more leaves on the same plant. Be sure that all three leaves are completely covered in plastic but that there are sufficient holes in the plastic so that air can reach the leaf.

Next, cut three half-inch squares from the black plastic. Using the same plant that already has three of its leaves completely encased in plastic, tape a black square onto the top of each of three large, healthy plant leaves. The small squares of the leaves will be deprived of sunlight.

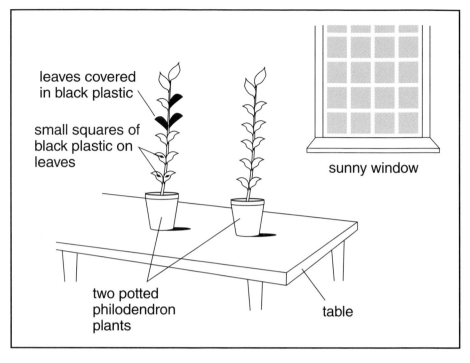

leaves covered in black plastic

small squares of black plastic on leaves

sunny window

two potted philodendron plants

table

How do leaves affect plant growth?

Put the plant in a sunny window. Put your control plant, which has no leaves covered, next to your experimental plant. Water the plants when the soil feels dry.

Observe both plants carefully for a month, recording the time, date, and what you see during each observation. What happened to the leaves that were completely covered in black plastic? Is one of the plants growing faster or looking healthier than the other? Do leaves fall off either plant?

Remove the squares of black plastic from the three leaves. What do you notice underneath? Record your observations in your notebook. What effect did depriving some part of the plant leaves of sunlight have on the leaves and the plant?

Further Explorations

Try this experiment by using plants other than philoden-dron. You might cover the leaves with foil instead of plastic material. Do different plants respond differently?

Investigation 18

Will artificial light stimulate plant growth?

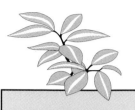

If you have done Investigation 17, where you covered some of a plant's leaves with plastic to block light, you learned whether or not depriving leaves of sunlight affected plant growth. When leaves cannot get light, photosynthesis cannot take place.

But what would happen if plants got extra light? What if, in addition to natural sunlight during the day, they also had artificial light at night?

Take a dozen dried peas and soak them in water overnight. The next morning, place the peas on double sheets of paper towels spread out to line a plastic box. Close the lid to keep the moisture in. Sprinkle the paper towels with water as needed, keeping them damp.

In a few days, the peas will sprout. Check often and write in your notebook the time, date, and what you observe happening to the seeds.

Once the peas have sprouted, choose three large sprouts and plant them in a small pot filled with potting soil. Put a piece of masking tape on it and label this pot A. Choose

Materials

* 12 dried peas
* a plastic box with lid (or a baking pan covered with plastic wrap)
* paper towels
* notebook and pen
* 2 small flowerpots
* potting soil
* masking tape
* water
* centimeter ruler
* fluorescent light

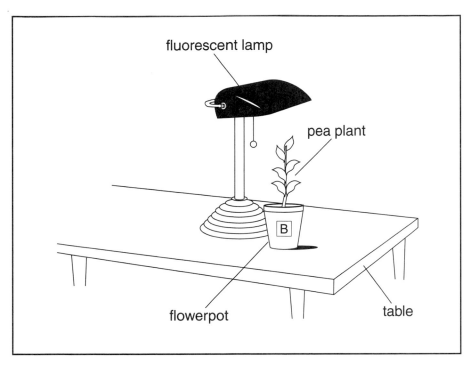

fluorescent lamp

pea plant

B

flowerpot

table

What is the effect of artificial light on growing plants?

another three healthy seedlings and plant them in a second pot. Use masking tape and a pen to label this pot B. Put the two pots side by side in a sunny window and water them when the soil feels dry.

Check the pots often, noting the time and date of each observation and what you observe. When the peas have sprouted from the soil, measure the new plants from the tip of the growth to the soil.

One week after plants have sprouted in both pots, move pot B each night into a room where it stays under a lighted fluorescent light. Put the plant within one foot of the light source. Each morning, move pot B back to its place next to pot A.

Continue to make frequent observations of the growth of the seedlings, noting the time, date, and what you saw and measured during each observation.

Which plants grew faster? Is there a difference in height, number of leaves, and color of leaves?

Further Explorations

If you try this experiment with incandescent light instead of fluorescent light, will the results be different? Can plants get too much light? What happens if you raise seedlings in the house under a fluorescent light and then you put them outside where they get full direct sunlight? Which plants grow faster? Is there a difference in height, number of leaves, and color of leaves?

Investigation 19

Can you observe water leaving a plant through its leaves?

Materials

* 3 small, healthy house plants such as philodendrons
* masking tape
* large, clear plastic bags
* twist ties
* measuring spoon or cup
* notebook and pen
* towel

The human body has a circulatory system to transport blood. Plants also have a transport system, and if you carried out Investigation 2, you learned that the movement of water in a plant is done through tubes called xylem.

Water also leaves plants, as you will learn from this experiment. The process by which water leaves the plants is called transpiration.

For this investigation, you will need three small, healthy house plants of the same species and size, planted in the same size pots. Philodendrons are a good choice. Each plant should have at least ten leaves.

Use a pen and masking tape to number the pots 1, 2, and 3. Remove all the leaves from plant 1. Wrap the stem and its pot in a large, clear plastic bag. Secure it tightly with a twist tie.

Remove half the leaves from plant 2, and wrap it as you did with plant 1.

Leave all the leaves on plant 3, and wrap it like the other two. Put the plants in a sunny spot.

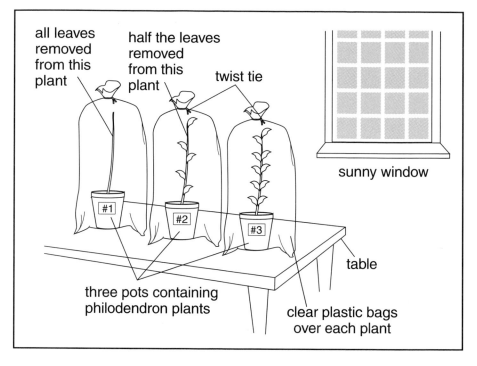

all leaves removed from this plant

half the leaves removed from this plant

twist tie

sunny window

#1

#2

#3

table

three pots containing philodendron plants

clear plastic bags over each plant

Observe transpiration.

Each night, carefully remove the plastic bags and note the amount of moisture trapped inside each plastic bag. If there is sufficient moisture, collect it in a measuring spoon or cup. Write down the time and date of your observation in your science notebook along with information about the amount of water observed or measured from each plant. Measure and give each plant the same amount of water every other night.

Dry the insides of each of the bags with a towel and put each of the three plants back inside their bags, securing them tightly with the twist tie.

Continue to follow this procedure each night for one week, recording the time, date, and information from each observation. Do plants lose measurable amounts of water through their leaves? Does the number of leaves affect the amount of water leaving the plant?

Further Explorations

You could investigate in more detail by putting one plant in a warm spot and another in a cool spot. Is there a difference in the amount of moisture released? Try putting one plant where it will get lots of direct sunlight and comparing the moisture collected with a plant that receives no direct sunlight. Do plants respond the same way under artificial light?

Investigation 20

Do different soils affect plant growth?

In the wild, seeds fall in many places and may grow in a number of different kinds of soil. Some kinds of soil hold moisture longer than others. If soil is packed down hard, perhaps in a place where people have walked over it, water may not penetrate the soil, and few plants will grow there. Water drains through sandy soil quickly and leaves it dry.

This experiment will help you determine whether different plant mediums result in different plant growth.

Materials

* 4 potted marigolds
* water
* masking tape
* potting soil
* backyard soil
* vermiculite
* centimeter ruler
* sand
* notebook and pen

Purchase four plants of similar size such as small, potted marigolds. Remove each of the four plants from their pots and gently rinse all the soil from their roots. You will be repotting each of these plants.

Put pieces of masking tape on each of the four pots and label them SAND, VERMICULITE, BACKYARD SOIL, and POTTING SOIL. Fill each pot with the appropriate planting medium and plant one of the marigolds in each.

Keep the four potted plants side by side in a sunny spot. When the soil feels dry, water all the plants with equal amounts of water.

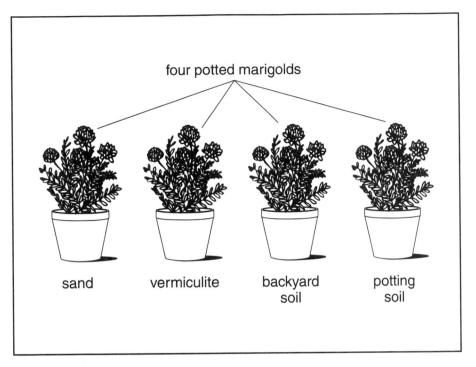

four potted marigolds

sand   vermiculite   backyard soil   potting soil

How do different soils affect plant growth?

Every other day for eight weeks, observe your plants. Write down the time and date of each observation and what you noticed. Note the growth of each plant by measuring from the soil to the top of the plant and by counting the number of buds or flowers and the number of leaves. Note the color and condition of the leaves.

Which plant was healthiest-looking (taller, fuller, with most flowers and dark green leaves) after eight weeks? Why is this?

Further Explorations

In some places, soil is compacted. What effect does that have on plant growth? In some places, soil is more acidic or alkaline. Devise an experiment to show the effect that acidity or alkalinity in soils might have on plant growth.

Investigation 21

Will roots respond to substances in the soil?

Plant roots serve three functions. They support the plant, draw food and water from the surrounding soil, and store food.

To find out whether roots will respond to various substances in the soil, you will need one small, healthy house plant in a two-inch pot, potting soil, and bone meal, which can be purchased from a plant nursery. Prepare an eight-inch pot in which you will repot your plant. First, jam a piece of cardboard box vertically into the pot. Fill half the pot with potting soil and leave the other half empty.

In a bucket, mix four parts potting soil with one part bone meal. Fill the empty side of the eight-inch pot with this mixture.

Put a strip of masking tape along the rim of the pot on the bone meal side and mark it BONE MEAL. Carefully remove the piece of cardboard that you used to divide the pot in half. Now plant your small house plant right in the center of the pot. Be sure to wash your hands thoroughly with soap and water after repotting your plant.

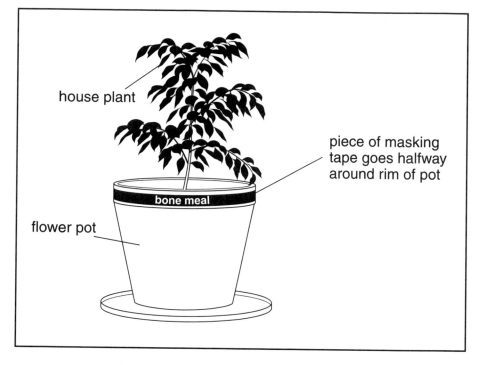

house plant

piece of masking tape goes halfway around rim of pot

bone meal

flower pot

Show the effect of bone meal on root growth.

Put the plant in a spot where it gets plenty of sunlight. Water your plant regularly when the soil feels dry.

Measure your plant from the soil to the top of the plant. Count its leaves. Note the time, date, and other information in your science notebook. Repeat this process once a week.

After six weeks, carefully remove the plant from its pot, being sure to note which side of the plant was planted in the bone meal. Gently wash the soil from its roots.

Study the root system carefully. Did more and thicker roots grow on the side of the pot that contained bone meal, or could you detect no differences in the two sides of the root system? Record the time, date, and your observations in your science notebook. You may want to photograph your results. Carefully replace your plant so that it can continue to grow.

Further Explorations

If you have a patch of lawn where you can experiment, you might try adding different substances to a patch of grass and observe the results. You might apply organic nitrogen to one patch in the form of cottonseed meal or soybean meal, or you could apply a dry or liquid inorganic fertilizer. Does the grass look different in the patches that you fertilized?

Investigation 22

How does a plant grow from an airborne seed?

Plants reproduce in many different ways. The most familiar form of plant reproduction is from a seed, and few seeds are more common than those of the dandelion. How does a plant such as a dandelion grow from an airborne seed?

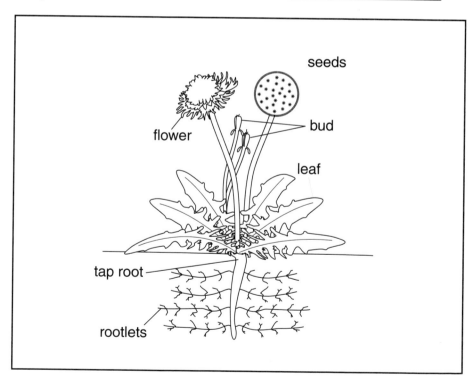

A dandelion plant has airborne seeds.

To prepare your "seed bed," gather lint from a clothes dryer and cover the bottom of a plastic box with it. Sprinkle it with water. (If clothes dryer lint is not available to you, use paper towels instead.)

After a dandelion flowers, it shrivels and stays closed until it opens to become a white seed puff. Find a dandelion that is in seed. Hold the dandelion seed puff above your prepared seed bed and gently blow so that the seeds become airborne and land inside the box.

Put the cover on the box and place the box in a sunny spot. Observe your seed bed each day. Note the time and date of each observation, as well as what you see.

The dandelion seeds will detach themselves from their parachutes and develop into seedlings. Observe your seedlings as they grow, and be sure to keep the lint or paper towels moist.

Further Explorations

Dandelions are common and are very adaptable plants. Look at dandelions that you find growing in different places. In a field of uncut grass, the dandelion will have a long stalk. In a lawn where the grass has been cut, the dandelion grows with a short flower stalk, and the leaves spread out flat. What other plants adapt and change when growing in different places?

Maple seeds are shaped like helicopter propellers. Try sprouting one of these seeds on damp paper towels. What happens to the parts of the seed?

Investigation 23

Will a vegetable reproduce from roots and stems?

Materials

* glass or plastic baking dish that is at least four inches deep
* 2 carrots
* 2 beets
* 2 parsnips
* knife
* marbles or pebbles
* water
* notebook and pen
* potato
* paper bag
* 8-inch flowerpot
* potting soil

You can grow new vegetables from roots and stems. To grow a new plant from a root, you must use a root that has lots of food stored in it. Good choices are carrots, beets, sweet potatoes, white potatoes, radishes, parsnips, and turnips.

First, you can try to reproduce vegetables in a dish garden. Use a glass or plastic baking dish that is at least four inches deep. You will need the leafy tops from three root vegetables such as beets, carrots, and parsnips.

Under adult supervision, carefully slice off the tops of two beets, two carrots, and two parsnips. Cut at about two inches down from the big end of the root. Remove any wilted leaves that may still be attached to the tops.

Fill the baking dish with pebbles or marbles to a depth of two to three inches. Then add water until it is within an inch of the top of the bowl. Take one of the tops of the vegetables and bury it partway beneath the pebbles or marbles. Move the stones around to hold the vegetable root in place.

Repeat this process with all the vegetables. Put the dish in a place where it will receive light but not direct sun for a few days. Then you can move it into a sunny spot. Add water as needed.

Check your vegetable garden often. In your notebook, record the time, date, and your observations. The carrot will grow new thin, feathery leaves out of the top. The beet leaves will be shaped somewhat like arrowheads. The parsnip will grow a long stem with pairs of opposite leaves.

Now try growing a vegetable from a stem. A white potato is a stem that grows underground. It contains stored food. Place a potato in a paper bag and store it in a warm place. Wait until several shoots sprout from the potato eyes.

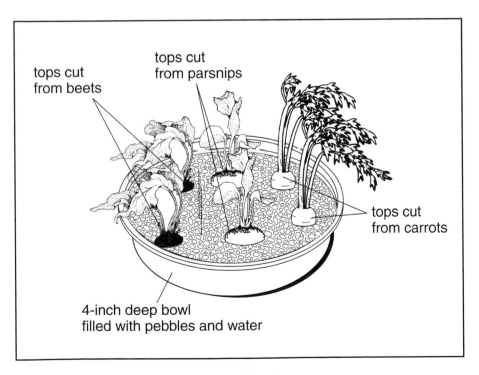

tops cut from beets

tops cut from parsnips

tops cut from carrots

4-inch deep bowl filled with pebbles and water

Grow new vegetables from roots.

Prepare an eight-inch pot by first putting some small pebbles in the bottom for drainage. Then fill the pot with rich potting soil.

Cut two pieces from the sprouting potato, making sure that there is an eye and a shoot in each piece. Plant the two pieces in your flowerpot with the sprouts pointing up. Place the pot in a warm, sunny spot. Water the plant when the soil feels dry.

Check on the potato plant often, and in your notebook, write the time and date and what you observe. Before long, your potato will be growing new stems and leaves. Continue to water as needed, make frequent observations, and write your observations in your notebook.

When the potato plant is about a foot high, take it outside and gently knock it out of its pot. If you check the soil around the roots carefully, you will be able to see small potatoes that have been forming under the soil. You can transplant these outdoors in your summer garden.

Further Explorations

You used carrots, beets, and parsnips in your dish garden. What other vegetables might work? Try these in a second garden. Some vegetables are dried. Try to devise an experiment showing dehydration and reconstitution of some vegetables.

Investigation 24

Can you grow new plants from leaves?

You can grow a plant not only from seeds, roots, and stems, but also from leaves. African violets are one of a number of plants that can be started from a leaf. Prepare a two-inch pot by filling it with vermiculite. Moisten the vermiculite with water.

Cut a leaf from an African violet plant, being sure to keep a part of the stem attached to the leaf. Use a pencil to make a hole in the moist vermiculite. Bury the stem part of the African violet leaf in the vermiculite. Gently press the vermiculite around the stem so that it stays upright.

Put a large, clean jar upside down over your potted plant to keep it moist. Add water to the vermiculite as needed to keep it moist but not soaking wet.

Observe the leaf often, writing in your notebook the time, date, and your observations. Before long, a new plant will begin to grow at the point where the stem meets the vermiculite. New roots will grow at the bottom of the stem.

The rex begonia is another wonderful plant to use in showing reproduction from a leaf. Under favorable conditions, the leaf of this plant will send out roots. Fleshy-leafed plants such as rex begonias store a considerable amount of food in the leaves.

With adult supervision, use a sharp knife to make a cut at each large vein of the begonia leaf. Fill a small bowl with damp vermiculite and place the cut leaf on the damp vermiculite with the underside down. Put a few pebbles on the leaf to hold it down flat.

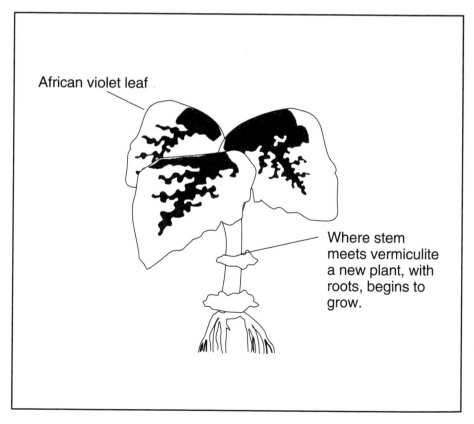

Root an African violet leaf in vermiculite.

Use a large, clear glass bowl to cover the smaller bowl containing the leaf on the vermiculite. This will help keep the leaf moist. Place the whole setup where the leaf will get light.

Observe the begonia leaf often, recording in your notebook the time and date of each observation and what you saw. Sprinkle the vermiculite with water as needed to keep it moist. In a few days, tiny new plants will form at each spot where you made the cut on the leaf.

When these new plants are about three inches tall, you can separate them from the original leaf and plant them into separate pots containing potting soil.

Further Explorations

Some plants will produce new plants if their leaves are placed in water. Experiment with different plants. Cut leaves from different plants and place them in water. Watch carefully over time. With which plants do roots begin to form at the base of the leaves?

Investigation 25

How do plants respond to light?

Materials

* potato

* paper bag

* notebook and pen

* glue

* miscellaneous cardboard pieces

* cardboard box with lid, about 18" x 10" x 6"

Plants respond to stimuli, but they move so slowly that we may not notice. A few, such as the sensitive plant *Mimosa pudica*, have leaves that fold and droop as soon as the surface is touched.

Sources of plant stimulation include gravity, touch, chemicals, and light. If a stimulus causes a response in a plant, the response is called a tropism. Phototropism, for example, is a response to light.

You may have built a maze to see if a mealworm, hamster, or gerbil can follow a path to food. To see if a plant can find its way through a maze to a light source, place a regular white potato in a paper bag in a warm, dark place. Check your potato every few days. In your notebook, record the time and date and what you see. Soon the eyes of the potato will be growing sprouts.

The sprouts grow quickly using food, in the form of starches, that is stored in underground stems called tubers. The potato plant is a perennial—it grows back year after year. It goes through the annual cycle of producing sprouts and flowers in spring, storing food in tubers during summer, dying back in autumn, and surviving underground during winter.

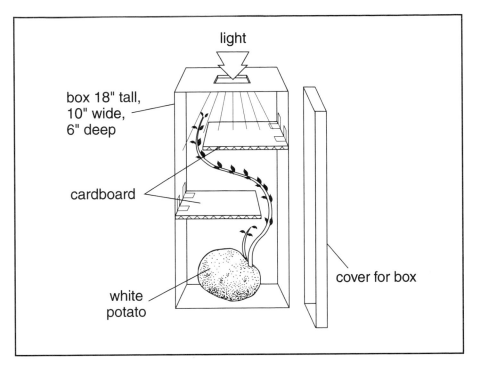

box 18" tall, 10" wide, 6" deep

light

cardboard

white potato

cover for box

Will a plant follow a maze to seek light?

To build a maze, glue cardboard pieces into place inside a cardboard box with a lid. The drawing on page 93 will help.

You will need several large pieces of cardboard to make the two screens within the cardboard box. (You could use oak tag if cardboard is not available.) Your finished maze will be about ten inches wide, eighteen inches long, and six inches deep. (These measurements need not be exact.)

Once you have finished your maze, place your sprouting potato in a corner of the box behind one of the cardboard screens. Close the lid. Stand the box on end with the potato at the bottom and the opposite side with the opening facing up and into the light. Put the box in a sunny spot.

Every other day, carefully open the maze and write down in your notebook the time, date, and your observations. Do not touch or move the potato.

Does the potato grow shoots that find their way through the maze, out of the opening of the box, and into the sunlight?

Further Explorations

Try constructing other mazes to see whether other vines, such as ivy, will grow through the maze to the light.

Glossary

chlorophyll—The green pigment in plants that is used in photosynthesis.

flower—The reproductive structure of a seed-bearing plant.

phloem—The part of the vascular system that moves nutrients through the plant.

photosynthesis—The process through which sunlight is turned into energy for the plant by the leaf, and oxygen is released into the air as a by-product.

pistil—The female organ on the flower that produces seeds for a plant.

pollination—Having the pollen from a flower's stamen come in contact with the pistil of the flower.

roots—The portion of a plant that is usually underground and that serves to support the plant.

stamen—The male organ on a flower that produces pollen.

stomata—Tiny openings in the outer layer of plant organs through which gases are exchanged.

transpiration—The loss of water vapor from plants, most of which occurs through the stomata.

vascular—Referring to the system of channels that convey nutrients throughout a plant.

vascular bundles—Bundles of tubes that run up and down the plant from the root system to the leaves.

xylem—The part of the vascular system that moves liquids from the roots to all parts of the plant and usually makes up the stem.

List of Suppliers

Acorn Naturalists
17300 E. 17th St., Ste. J-236, Tustin, CA 92780
(714) 838-4888, (800) 422-8886
Fax: (714) 838-5869, (800) 452-2802

Ben Meadows
3589 Broad St., Atlanta, GA 30341
(770) 455-0907, (800) 241-6401
Fax: (800) 628-2068

Carolina Biological Supply Co.
2700 York Rd., Burlington, NC 27216
(910) 584-0381, (800) 334-5551

Fisher Scientific
485 S. Frontage Rd., Educational Materials Division, Burr Ridge, IL 60521
(708) 655-4410, (800) 955-1177

Forestry Suppliers
P.O. Box 8397, Jackson, MS 39284-8397
(601) 354-3565, (800) 647-5368
Fax: (800)543-4203

National Gardening Association
180 Flynn Ave., Burlington, VT 05401
(802) 863-1308, (800) 863-5962

Young Naturalist Co.
1900 N. Main, Newton, KS 67114
(316) 283-4103
Fax: (316) 283-9108

Further Reading

Bates, Jeffrey W. *Seeds to Plants: Projects with Biology.* Danbury, Conn.: Franklin Watts, Inc., 1991.

Beller, Joel. *Experimenting with Plants.* New York: Simon & Schuster Trade, 1985.

Bleifeld, Maurice. *Adventures with Biology.* Springfield, N.J.: Enslow Publishers, Inc., 1997.

Bourgeois, Paulette. *Amazing Dirt Book.* Reading, Mass.: Addison Wesley Longman, Inc., 1990.

Brennan, Georgeanne, and Ethel Brennan. *Children's Kitchen Garden: A Book of Gardening, Cooking, & Learning.* Berkeley, Calif.: Ten Speed Press, 1997.

Catherall, Ed. *Exploring Plants.* Chatham, N.J.: Raintree Steck-Vaughn, 1992.

Dietl, Ulla. *The Plant-and-Grow Project Book.* New York: Sterling Publishing Company, Inc., 1995.

Durant, Penny R. *Exploring the World of Plants.* New York: Franklin Watts, Inc., 1995.

Fell, Derek. *Kid's First Book of Gardening—With Kit.* Philadelphia: Running Press, 1989.

Gardner, Robert. *Science Project Ideas About Trees.* Springfield, N.J.: Enslow Publishers, Inc., 1997.

———. *Science Projects About Plants.* Springfield, N.J.: Enslow Publishers, Inc., 1999.

Gibbons, Gail. *From Seed to Plant.* New York: Holiday House, 1991.

Goldenberg, Janet. *Weird Things You Can Grow.* New York: Random House Books for Young Readers, 1994.

Hershey, David R. *Plant Biology Science Projects.* New York: John Wiley and Sons, Inc., 1995.

Hill, Joan and Gwen. *Goodship. African Violets: The Complete Guide.* North Pomfret, Vt.: Trafalgar Square, 1998.

Hunken, Jorie. *Botany for All Ages: Discovering Nature Through Activities for Children & Adults.* Second edition. Old Saybrook, Conn.: Globe Pequot Press, 1994.

Jennings, Terry. *Flowers.* Danbury, Conn.: Children's Press, 1989.

Joly, Dominique, Philippe Joly, and Nathalie Co. *How Does Your Garden Grow?* New York: Sterling Publishing Company, 1996.

Kerrod, Robin. *Plants in Action.* New York: Marshall Cavendish Corp., 1990.

Lerner, Carol. *Cactus.* New York: Morrow Jr. Books, 1992.

Madgwick, Wendy. *Cacti & Other Succulents.* Chatham, N.J.: Raintree Steck-Vaughn, 1990.

———. *Flowering Plants.* Chatham, N.J.: Raintree Steck-Vaughn, 1990.

———. *Fungi & Lichens.* Chatham, N.J.: Raintree Steck-Vaughn, 1990.

Miller, Christina G., and Louise Berry. *Air Alert: Rescuing the Earth's Atmosphere.* Old Tappan, N.J.: Simon & Schuster Children's, 1996.

Miller, Susanna. *Beans & Peas.* Minneapolis: The Lerner Publishing Group, 1990.

Morgan, Nina. *Plant Cycle.* New York: Thompson Learning, 1993.

Pascoe, Elaine. *Seeds & Seedlings.* Woodbridge, Conn.: Blackbirch Press, Inc., 1997.

Parker, Steve. *Plants.* Tarrytown, N.Y.: Marshall Cavendish Corp., 1996.

Pearce, Querida L. *Wondrous Plant & Earth Experiments.* New York: Tor Books, 1990.

Rapp, Joel. *Let's Get Growing: Twenty-Five Quick & Easy Gardening Projects for Kids*. New York: Crown Publishing Group, Inc., 1993.

Reading, Susan. *Desert Plants*. New York: Facts on File, 1990.

Robson, Denny. *Grow It for Fun: Hands-On Projects*. Danbury, Conn.: Franklin Watts, Inc., 1991.

Roth, Charles Edmund. *The Amateur Naturalist: Explorations and Investigations*. Danbury, Conn.: Franklin Watts, Inc., 1993.

Smolinski, Jill. *50 Nifty Super Science Fair Projects*. Los Angeles: Lowell House Juvenile, 1996.

Suzuki, David T. *Looking at Plants*. New York: John Wiley and Sons, Inc., 1992.

Tant, Carl. *Seeds, Etc.* Angelton, Tex.: Biotech Publishing, 1992.

Taylor, Barbara. *Growing Plants*. Danbury, Conn.: Franklin Watts, Inc., 1991.

———. *Green Thumbs Up!: The Science of Growing Plants*. New York: Random House Books for Young Readers, 1992.

Tesar, Jenny E. *Green Plants*. Woodbridge, Conn.: Blackbirch Press, Inc., 1993.

VanCleave, Janice P. *Janice VanCleave's Plants: Mind-Boggling Experiments You Can Turn into Science Fair Projects*. New York: John Wiley and Sons, Inc., 1996.

Walker, Lois. *Get Growing! Exciting Plant Projects for Kids*. New York: John Wiley and Sons, Inc., 1991.

Williams, John. *Autumn Science Projects*. Parsippany, N.J.: Julian Messner, 1996.

———. *Spring Science Projects*. Parsippany, N.J.: Julian Messner, 1997.

Winckler, Suzanne, and Mary M. Rodgers. *Our Endangered Planet: Soil*. Minneapolis: Lerner Publishing Group, 1993.

Wood, Robert W. *Science for Kids: Thirty-Nine Easy Plant Biology Experiments*. Blue Ridge Summit, Pa.: TAB Books, 1991.

Woodward, John. *Our Food*. Milwaukee: Gareth Stevens Publishers, Inc., 1997.

Internet
Addresses

"Desert Plant Survival." *Desert USA.* August 24, 1998. <http://www.desertusa.com/du_plantsurv.html> (September 25, 2000).

Gallawa, J. Carlton. "Microwaves: How Dangerous Are They?" *Complete Microwave Oven Repair and Information Network.* 1989–1997. <http://www.gallawa.com/microtech/mwdanger.html> (September 25, 2000).
Provides information on how microwaves work.

Jauron, Richard. "Growing Geraniums From Seed." *Horticulture & Home Pest News.* January 5, 1998. <http://www.ipm.iastate.edu/ipm/hortnews/1995/1-13-1995/geran.html> (September 25, 2000).
Gives tips on growing geraniums from seeds.

Kendrick, Bill. "Pea Experiment." *"Pea Soup" The Story of Mendel.* 1996. <http://www.sonic.net/~nbs/projects/anthro201/exper> (September 25, 2000).

Lanham, Keith. "Bibliography of African Violet Sources." *African Violets on the Cheap.* n.d. <http://www.netusa1.net/~klanham/biblio.html> (September 25, 2000).
A bibliography of sources that explore the growth,
propagation, and display of African violets.

Purdue University. "Pineapple." *Welcome to NewCROP the New Crop Resource Online Program.* July 2, 1996. <http://www.hort.purdue.edu/newcrop/Crops/pineapple.html> (September 25, 2000).
Information on pineapple plants.

Trent, J. "Our Students' Projects." *TENET.* n.d. <http://www-tenet. cc.utexas.edu/minigrants/antoine/p4.html> (September 25, 2000).
An experiment using potting soil versus sand to grow bean sprouts.

Virginia Carolina Peanuts. "Educational Materials." *Virginia Carolina Peanuts.* n.d. <http://aboutpeanuts.com/educ.html> (September 25, 2000).
Information about peanuts.

Index